Horace's Diary

A pony in lockdown

CAROLYN MORGAN

Thanks

Thank you to David my boyfriend, for giving me Horace as a foal.
Sarah, my great friend, who helped take the photos.
Annemarie Young, who knows what you have to do to publish a book.
Andy Wilson for the design of the front cover and insides.

And not forgetting the star of the book, the wonderful Horace, his
bestest friend Crosswell Rufus, and of course, Birtie, my assistant.

Carolyn Morgan,
Crosswell Riding Stables

ISBN 978-1-915292-67-4

Published by Crosswell Publishing (www.crosswellridingtrekking.co.uk)

Designed by Andy Wilson for Green Desert Ltd

Edited by Annemarie Young

Printed in the UK by Biddles Books Ltd.

Horace's Diary
A pony in lockdown

Me when I was
6 months old!

A message from Horace's friend, Carolyn

I started writing Horace's diary to help everyone keep in touch with the stables, during the first lockdown. Little did I know that it would end in a book!

I hope you all enjoy reading about Horace and his friends: his adventures, and life at the stables during lockdown.

Whether you're an adult or a child, I hope this book brings a smile to your face.

Hello, my name is Ceulan Horace. I was born in 2016 on 26th April. My dad is called Ceulan Calon Lan, he was supreme champion at the Royal Welsh show! My mum is Mynyddtarren Hermina and she is very beautiful. I live with Carolyn at her Crosswell stables with lots of my pony friends. Each day, I intend to write a diary about my training because my owner Carolyn seems to have a lot of time on her hands lately.

Good morning. This is my friend Rufus. His dad is called Penstrumbly Sax Mad Johnny, (hope I spelt that right!). He is a Welsh cob. His mum is called Crosswell Roxanna, Roxy to her friends. She's had 14 foals, yes 14 foals!! She is 25 years old this year and looks after Mixi, who is slighter older than her. Rufus's brothers and sisters all do activities like showing (Crosswell Caitlyn in particular), hunting and jumping (Crosswell Mayflower, Crosswell Duds and Crosswell Harry).

I asked Rufus had he done anything like that? He said that when he was growing up, he was always called names, like Big Head and Short Legs, which he found upsetting. He said that Carolyn has always said that in her eyes he is beautiful and that's great with him. In my eyes he's my hero, because he's always giving me great words of wisdom and helping me.

Today, I learnt to go round and round in circles. Apparently, it's called lunging. It's for me to get used to my saddle and bridle and word commands, without having anyone sitting on my back.

I thought I'd better introduce some of my stable mates to you (some are nicer than others!). This is Beauty. She's horrible to me. I'm scared of her – all she does is put her ears back at me, and she makes horrible squeaky noises whenever I try to make friends. My bestest friend Rufus tells me not to worry, she used to do that to him when he was my age. He said it's because she is the oldest one here (and she looks it, he he!). Rufus said she has to put everyone in their place. That's mean. But Rufus says I will learn. I wonder if I'll be going round and round in circles again for my training today?

So exciting, I went out on the roads today for a walk with anther pony called Pie. Lots of things to see and explore. Apparently, Rufus says that you can get lost if you go out there on your own. I can't wait.

Carolyn has been showing me the stable's Facebook page. I can't believe so many people are interested in my diary! To tell you the truth I'm a little nervous because I can see my DAD and relations are reading it. I will try my best not to disgrace the family. But as Rufus has told me, you can't believe all that's posted on Facebook, so I might leave out the days when I don't want to listen to Carolyn, and only include my very well-behaved days.

I'm waiting patiently for Carolyn to start today's exercises. All she seems to be doing these days is cleaning tack. I've never seen her do that before!

Poor brave Rufus. He didn't tell me his hoof was hurting. He has been hurting for lots of nights, ever since he played tag with me. He was playing with me to cheer me up, as I had just left my winter buddy, Ceulan Socyn. He said he must have trodden on a stone because it really hurt and it's been getting worse every day. I had wondered why Carolyn kept on looking at his hoof and doing something. But today a doctor called Grant came and made him better. Rufus said if you want a job doing properly you must get an experienced person. I don't think he thinks Carolyn was up to the job.

Oh dear, I've made a mistake,
he was a blacksmith not a doctor.

All I've done today is have my saddle and bridle on. How boring is that. All Carolyn did was stand on a step above me. I have heard people saying something about 'six foot' all week. Do you think they were telling her to stand six foot above me? I must say it gave me a bit of a fright when she first did it, but then I just started dreaming of going to all those shows that Rufus has told me about. He went to Nevern show last year and won a rosette! I do hope I can be like him.

Rufus will not get out of bed this morning. He said we can stay in bed an hour extra today. I thought Carolyn told us yesterday we would lose an hour in bed, but who am I to argue? I have always been taught to respect and listen to my elders, although sometimes I do wonder.

Like this for instance. The other day, grumpy Beauty made faces at me when I was doing my exercises with Carolyn. I told Rufus that night and he said her bark is worse than her bite. Now, firstly ponies do not bark (that dog that's always following Carolyn does), and secondly, she can't bite because she's lost all her teeth! This is what I mean, listen to your elders?

My lesson today was long reining. Carolyn stood behind me with two bits of string attached to my bridle, and Sarah, Buster's owner (he's king of the big horse herd), led me around. It was very odd having Carolyn behind me. I kept looking back at her, wondering what she was up to back there. We went round the yard, up the bank, round the school, round the yard, up the bank, round the school round the yard... THEN out on the road!

That was a little more interesting to tell you the truth. We went up and up – what a climb! – then round a corner (such a long way from home) then we turned round. I got braver and braver when I knew we were going home. Half way down the hill, Sarah stood behind with Carolyn. I got scared. I was on my own, with no one in front (except that dog again). Carolyn told me to keep going, telling me I could do it. I didn't want to let her down, so I just walked. The further I went, the more confident I became. Wait till I tell Rufus, he will be so impressed!

We must have been gone for hours. I must say that I'm a little tired now, but what an adventure. When I told Rufus, he came and scratched my back, which I love. I will sleep well tonight, dreaming of tomorrow's lesson.

TWINS!

Carolyn put a saddle and bridle on Rufus and on me. AND we had the same coloured thing that goes under the saddle! I pretend he's my big brother. I know we're not blood relations, but he looks out for me. He tells me wise things and always listens to my stories, and he tells me how well I've done. He gives me such confidence, I sometimes feel I can jump and do anything.

Although, I do think about my blood family a lot. Some of them I've never met, but through my diary, long lost relatives have contacted me. It's great as it gives me a lovely warm feeling that I belong. My brother, Ceulan Hannibal, and his owner, Mia Louise, got in touch – he's the same colour as me! I told Rufus and he was pleased for me. He said he'd lost touch with lots of his brothers and sisters, which is sad. But don't get me wrong, I'm part of a HUGE family here and that's great.

Rufus is teaching me to get used to having weight on my back. He said it was my homework.

Rufus also told me that he teaches humans. He learnt it from his mother, Roxy, when he was growing up. When he was in the stable sometimes with his mother, she would kick the door with her front foot, and somebody would either come over and give her a treat or a pat. When they walked away, she would do it again and guess what? They came back again!

But he said Carolyn never learns, she either takes him out of the stable and puts him in a stall, where it's difficult to kick with his front foot, or puts him in the naughty corner. Rufus is so clever. Although the naughty corner does sound frightening.

What fun today! Carolyn and I (and that dog too who goes everywhere) went for a walk in a huge wood and I jumped over a huge fallen down tree, but when we came back to the stables, Carolyn lay on top of me and tried to squash me! Now, I'm not sure if she had a very big supper last night and ate all the pies, because I really felt her up there. Thank goodness Rufus gave me that lesson and homework last night, it worked well. 'Plant each leg out as far as you can, and just stand there like a square,' he said, and it worked. Easy when you know how.

Well, I've heard of goat yoga but pony yoga? Goodness knows what Carolyn is calling this movement. I would hate to hazard a guess. I'm sure this must be Carolyn's daily workout, but I've no idea what this has to do with my training.

After all that nonsense, we went out on the road long reining. She pulled an old branch from the hedge and started dragging it behind her. It made a terrible noise and gave me a huge fright to start with, then I got used to it. I overheard Carolyn saying it was training for the trap, so I would get used to lots of different noises behind me.

What's a trap? Rufus will know.

Today is the first time in my whole life that someone has sat on me. Rufus was so proud when I told him. The night before, he'd told me that it's much easier to have an upright human on your back, rather than one that lies across you or leans from side to side. Your balance is better. He was right (when is Rufus ever wrong?). I found it so easy that it didn't bother me at all. I even stood to have my photo taken so I can show all my friends. I will remember this day for the rest of my life.

Today we went for a walk down the road (no cars at the moment, so I can't get used to them). Carolyn dragged a branch behind her again, which made a terrible noise, but I didn't bother (ready for 'the trap'?). She's given that up now, and said she'll find something noisier. Bring it on!

Haven't left the field today. I don't know why. Carolyn and David were fencing so I decided I'd help them. I picked up the hammer and moved various other things for them. I'm sure they were very grateful for my help. (Apparently, David had something to do with me as a foal, but I can't remember that far back. I'll have to ask.)

Embarrassing. Degrading. I bet none of my family has ever had to do this before! Saddle bags are for pack horses, or even DONKEYS! I just might throw my toys out of the pram. (I've done that once before, but that's another story.) Oh no, here come Rufus and Beauty, what are they going to say?

Oh dear, I got it all wrong. I got a bit of a talking to from Rufus. He told me to stop being such a stuck up snob. He said that without pack horses and donkeys we wouldn't have been able to conquer lands and win wars, and humans wouldn't be able to earn a living so they could look after their families.

Today I've learnt a big lesson: no pony is better than the next pony.

I'm starting to learn that there's always a reason why Carolyn is teaching me a particular lesson. Take yesterday for example. I thought by putting those saddle bags on me she was trying to make me the laughing stock of the stables, but no, the saddle bags came in useful today. We went shopping in Brynberian. I long reined all the way there – it was miles. Bread, that people had ordered, arrived in a van. It was very strange because although everyone knew each other, they all stood a big distance from one another. And no one came to pat me, they just shouted from a distance, saying how wonderful I looked. I carried the bread home in my saddle bags with pride. I don't know how Carolyn could have done without me.

I must say that when I got home, my legs were tired, and I had a lie down in the field with my best friend Rufus. It's great having such a friend to chat to, so I can tell him about my adventures of the day. He said he's never carried bread for Carolyn, but he also wondered, on a slightly worrying note, if she's going to eat ALL that bread herself?

I would like to
introduce to you
my relation. I'm not
going to tell you
how I am related,
just that we are.
Her name is Ceulan
Heidi. Her mum
is Mynyddtarren

Hermia, and her dad is Ceulan Calib (he's very handsome
by all accounts). Heidi and her friend Ceulan Candy
arrived here about three months ago. They had preferential
treatment. They lived in a special stable, had special
bucket food, were put out in a special field (on their own),
and they wore special rugs! When news came that all the
shows had been cancelled, the rugs were off, they ate the
same food as us, and were turned out of their stable and
had to mix with us riff raff.

What a come down, thinking you were going to all
these top shows (Windsor was talked about), and then
disappointment. They will get over it, Rufus says, they are
young and their lives are in front of them.

Today I did slaloms and show jumping. I'm learning new
words ready for 'the trap'. To turn left is 'come', to turn
right is 'by' – or is it the other way around? I'm a bit
confused by it all at the moment. But I know tonight Rufus
will give me homework to help me get ready for tomorrow
(that's if I will be doing left and right tomorrow). It's
always something different, which I suppose is not boring.

Oh what a terrible, frightening day! It all started so well, with the sun shining, we were going on a different route to post a letter. On the way there, we passed some ponies in a field. There were two very small ones, who ran alongside the hedge making some very strange high pitched squeals. I was amazed at them as I had never heard anything like it, but I carried on. We posted the letter and turned for home.

When we were passing the field again, the ponies did the same thing, but one of them was so small it climbed UNDER the fence! It was awful, it was like those black devils your parents tell you about to scare you when you're naughty. They tell you the devils will chase you and catch you. Well, it did! The black devil jumped on my back, then turned and kicked out with both hind legs, squealing all the time. It was awful.

Carolyn was so brave. She hit it with the twig she carries. She shouted at it, grabbed my bridle and ran with me back to the owner's house with the black devil following. The owners caught it eventually and Carolyn led me home. 'That dog' came to my aid too, he tried to help by chasing it away, but Carolyn told him to stop in case the black devil turned on him.

I will never call him 'that dog' again. His name is Birtie. Carolyn had to lead me home because I got scared when she was behind me, but as we came nearer to home, I was fine about Carolyn and 'that dog', I mean Birtie, being behind me. When I got home, Rufus knew something was wrong. He told me that if ever you are scared or worried, always talk to your mum or dad or a good friend and it will help. And I must say that I feel so much better for telling Rufus. I hope there are no more letters to post tomorrow.

Something else

I thought I would tell you about a very strange ritual Carolyn does on a Thursday night, at eight o'clock. (I don't think she'll mind my telling you – and well, if she does it's too late now.) She puts Rufus and Nina in a stable and starts clapping her hands, which makes Rufus and Nina kick the doors. Rufus told me that Nina's owner works as a nurse in ITU in Carmarthen, and by kicking the doors we are copying Carolyn who is thanking the NHS. No idea what all these letters mean but they must be right because Rufus told me.

This is my favourite part of the day. A lovely massage. It sets me up to take on any adventures that may befall me throughout the day.

Last night when Rufus and I were having a chat before bed about my frightening day, he said that today had been a day of learning, and I will learn a lot from it. He said that I had not hurt myself, Birtie was fine and so was Carolyn. Always remember the best things – like my massage, eating grass, meeting new friends – this will always outweigh the frightening things. Also, you have an adventure to tell everyone.

So, my lesson today was uneventful (good news). We went long reining around the stables, with Carolyn using the words she's teaching me. I stop now (most of the time) when she says 'whoa'. When she picks up my hoof, she says 'up' and I lift up my hoof. But I'm still mixed up about left and right.

Rufus told me to go into the tack room for my surprise. He said Carolyn had just gone into her house (don't know how he knew that, he's so clever), and it was safe to sneak into the tack room. Rufus told me to go to the back and look up. I can't believe what I saw, my very own name plate ready for my bridle to be hung up on – I have arrived! I was so proud

to have my very own bridle hook. Of course, Rufus knew, that's why he sent me into the tack room. I was ecstatic that I was now part of the stables. No longer would I borrow somebody else's bridle, I would have my very own.

After I came down from my excitement, I realised it was not my full name, Ceulan Horace, so I asked Rufus why this was. He said that we all have our proper names on our passports. Passports are for everyone to know where we were born and our parents' names (if known, he said quietly), and if we want to go on holiday or to a show you have to take your passport with you. (Although this year we can't go to shows or on holiday.) On the passport it will have your full name, that's if you have come from a proper home (it seems Rufus can be a bit of a snob at times). Some of the horses have very long names that are very hard to pronounce, so they have nicknames. For example, Tommy's proper name is Camars Bart, Tiggy's is Rhydycar Ripple, and Rhydian's is Panteryrod Rhydian. That's why your full name is not put up. It would be confusing for everyone!

Carolyn and I went for a lovely walk up the road today. We stopped at a load of stones and I ate the delicious grass. I can now eat, no problem, with my bit in my mouth. At first it was impossible, but Rufus told me how to master it and I have. Problem is that my bit is now green instead of shiny silver. Never mind, Carolyn can clean it.

I thought I would gradually introduce you to everyone at the stables. First of all, Beauty. I used to be so scared of her because she used to make horrible faces at me. But now I have learnt to admire and respect her. Rufus says she is the matriarch. She has taught so many children to ride (that's my dream). Her owner, Emma, learnt to hunt, go to shows and all that sort thing on Beauty. She is old BUT her hearing is excellent. Beauty can be up in the back field, but when Carolyn opens the feed room door (it makes a distinctive noise when opened), she hears the door open and heads very quickly to the feed room, demanding food, which she gets!

She is the only one that can get away with that. She looks like a walking rug, but she doesn't care about her appearance. All the birds land on her, to take her hair for their nests. But she does get to have a massage every day. I expect that when all her woolly coat comes out, she will look half the size. I understand now that you must have

a strong, experienced leader to follow and learn from, and someone to put you in your place when you get a bit big for your shoes. Beauty does this job very well.

I asked Rufus when children will be able to ride me, and why is it that only Carolyn sits on my back? Rufus told me it would be a while yet as I had so much to learn. I said I know nearly everything now. Rufus laughed and said you will never stop learning. I'm amazed because I thought Rufus knew everything. Rufus said that for me to have a child on my back, I have to be more experienced than the child, so that I can show them what to do. Rufus said that at the stage I'm at in my education just now, I'm in primary school. When I get the knowledge and experience at university level then I'll be able to have children on my back. Rufus said he knows  that I wouldn't intentionally scare children, but unless you understand what children are capable of, it's better to have an experienced rider to show you the ropes.

I guess that's why it's so important for me to have Rufus as my mentor and leader, and for Carolyn to ride me. As long as she doesn't eat all her Easter eggs, I'll be able to cope – although I'm not sure about jumping big jumps with Carolyn on my back!

You'll never guess what happened to me today! I've got new front shoes. First time ever in my life. The man who put my new shoes on is called Grant. His other job is as an actor – he makes lots of Christmas videos under the name of 'Pappa G' (sounds more like a rapper to me). I was very brave, smoke came out from my hoof but it didn't hurt. Then Ifan put on some very shiny new shoes. Carolyn stood and held me because she has nothing better to do. Next time I'll not need any help ... possibly?

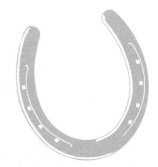

This is my new friend, Timothy. He's ridden by children (lucky him). Rufus tells me he likes the girl ponies and horses. Rufus said that in the spring he likes to herd the girls up in the field and keep them to himself. Some put up with him because they think he's handsome, and they like the attention, but others don't like the look of him, so they kick their heels up and run away. Apparently, one horse, called Kinvara, loves him. I can't understand it myself – she's

big, I mean really big, (Timothy is quite small) and she's very pretty, but I guess she must think he has a nice personality or something. I bet he would never dare go anywhere Beauty!

Today Carolyn put different tack on me. It went all the way round my body and even under my tail! Apparently, I will have another bridle. I wonder if I will be known as 'Horace two bridles'? Rufus said that it's called a driving harness.

I asked, 'What, would I be driving?' 'No,' he said, 'You'll be pulling a trap.' (There's that word again.) No doubt I'll be introduced to a 'trap' soon. If I'm pulling something, that means no one will be riding me. I'll become a multi-functional pony!

So that's a trap. Rufus said that this trap belongs to Teddy, and it's too big for me. Rufus thinks mine is kept in the bottom shed and it's the one Benny used to use. I said I didn't know that Teddy had his own trap, because I thought he taught children to ride. Rufus told me that when Teddy moved here from his last house, he brought his trap and harness with him. 'Where did he come from?' I asked. Apparently, it was Carolyn's very good friends, Jon and Gerald from Cimla, near Neath, who sorted it out.

'Did you know,' Rufus said, 'that they're teaching Carolyn to drive the trap?' 'Really,' I said, 'I thought Carolyn knew everything about ponies!' Rufus told me that sometimes Carolyn thinks she does. She gets carried away, tries to drive her trap too fast, and comes unstuck!

'Wow, tell me more about what happened,' I said.

Rufus said maybe he'd tell me the story after she's taught me how to pull a trap safely. 'No, I want to know now, PLEASE?' But Rufus said that some things are better not said. What does he mean, I wonder?

What a terrible fright I had this morning when Rufus
and I wandered in for breakfast. I thought that
my second cousins twice removed had died of some
terrible thing. Rufus assured me that youngsters
sleep an awful lot, play and eat, then sleep again.
I think that's what Carolyn is doing these days,
without the play.

I'm a very lucky pony. I've had three new things this week.
A new bridle. New shoes. A new hair style.

Cocoa was making such a fuss when Rufus and I walked
into the yard. 'Look what's happened to my beautiful mane,'
she said. Now, we all know what a drama queen Cocoa is,
but I must say her mane did look short. Cocoa said, 'When
I gallop over the mountains (walk more like it), I won't feel
the wind in my mane.' (That's
true.)

Rufus said that she'll get over
it. It will be some other drama
tomorrow so that she's the
centre of attention.

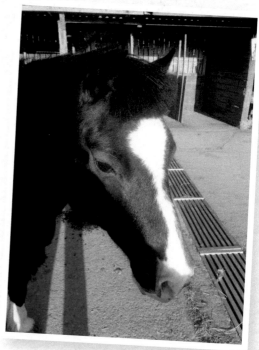

Let me introduce you to my friend Tommy. His proper name is Cemaes Bart. His dad was called Revel Status, which is such a fancy name. Tommy is not the sort of pony to brag about it – just as he never tells anyone how big he can jump, but we've all seen a picture of him. Tommy is a Welsh mountain pony like me, but I've noticed we're different. He has very, very small ears and big, beautiful eyes, where I do not.

When Tommy was a foal, he was sold at Cardigan pony sales. He was then advertised for sale at a horse food shop. Carolyn saw the advert, went to see him and brought him home. Tommy was five years old. He's now 12 years old. Rufus told me that for two winters Tommy went all the way to England to go hunting rabbits. I don't think he eats them – well, I haven't seen him anyway.

Tommy is the smallest pony here. He has the most distinctive neigh, you know it's him before you see him. He has taught lots of children to ride and has his photo taken all the time. He loves children and told me he's missing them very much at the moment. Poor Tommy.

Oh, the grass is so sweet and lush, the flowers smell so nice, and I've even noticed how beautiful Cocoa and Smartie are. I can see now why Timothy thinks Kinvara is the bees knees. The sun on my back – life is so good. Spring is definitely here. Ah, I can see Carolyn and Birtie coming to get me for my daily lesson. I don't feel like it today, why should I go? Carolyn can't make me. I'll tell her now. I'm just not doing it.

Oh dear, dear, what have I done. I just don't know what came over me. Rufus told me not to eat such sweet grass as it would lead me into trouble. At the time, I thought he was talking a load of rubbish. How can such a lovely bit of grass affect how I feel? But he was right. It didn't happen straight away, but oh dear something did happen, it made my head go all funny.

I feel very embarrassed and ashamed about the whole affair. I didn't know Carolyn could shout! We had a little discussion to start with, then I came round to seeing her way of thinking. At the end of our lesson, she gave me a big pat and offered me some grass, but I wasn't falling for that trick, so I politely refused. Rufus was very good when I returned. He looked up, said hello, and got back to eating. Later on, Beauty and Rufus were talking, and I heard them say that I'd got too big for my own boots (although I wear shoes), but I was back on track now and had learnt my lesson.

THURSDAY

23

APRIL

Birtie, Carolyn and I went for a little ride up the road today. Yesterday's little mishap was put behind us. What a lovely day it is today.

Today we went for a walk through the bluebell wood. It was so pretty. Rufus told me that it's part of the pub ride. Apparently, they ride to two pubs, the riders go into each pub for a drink of water while the horses eat the grass. Rufus said that after the riders have had their second drink of water, they ride so much better. And sometimes they go very fast up this track! Rufus said it's great fun because you get to eat a lot of grass. I asked Rufus if I could go on one, but he said I had to be a bit older.

This is one of my friends, Cappuccino. He has two bright blue eyes, which doesn't bother him now. But he told me that when he was growing up, he didn't like it because when some of the children came to ride him, they said his eyes scared them. It made him feel bad. But lots of children loved his eyes, they said they were beautiful eyes. So as he grew older, he learnt just to listen to the good things and everything improved. He thought 'Well, if I'm the best pony to ride, they'll overlook my eyes', and do you know what? It worked!

Carolyn bought Cappuccino from Cardigan pony sales when he was three years old and he has lived here many years. He never likes to be clean – if there's any mud to roll in, he finds it. On Own a Pony days he doesn't like to be groomed because he loves to stay scruffy. But when Rhian (who really owns him, he's the love of her life) used to take him to a show he looked so smart. I've seen pictures of him. He's the only pony who's really happy at the moment because he lives with Rhian and she goes to chat to him every day. It makes him feel so special.

Good morning. Horace is having a lie in today, so I apologise but it's me today. I just wanted to thank everyone who's been following Horace's progress. In these strange times we are all doing different things. I would never have dreamt that Horace would have the time or inclination to write a diary.

Thank you for all your lovely comments. It's amazing the number of people who follow his diary, from all over the world. I'm not sure when it will end because Horace seems to have a lot to say and so many more adventures to experience. I hope everyone is keeping well and sane.

This is a picture that Rufus showed me. He said that he goes riding on these mountains lots of times. He said it's beautiful up there. And do you know what? He heard a cuckoo yesterday. I so want to go there. Rufus said that anything is possible if you put your mind to it, but take it slowly and you will get there. I'm going to ride on those mountains one day. It's lovely to have a goal.

Birtie, Carolyn and I went for a little early morning ride before the rain came. We were riding along the road when in the field next to us, came running what I thought were lots of Majors and Jemmas. (They're horses that live at the stables and are coloured black and white.)

I had a bit of a fright – I couldn't believe my eyes. I put my head up, turned round to face home and wanted to run. But Carolyn stepped off me, gave me a big pat and turned my head to look at them. How stupid I was, they were baby cows not horses! We stared at one another over the wall. Carolyn said they hadn't seen a pony before, and they were very interested in me.

After I'd got over my initial shock, I ate some cow parsley, which is Major's favourite food, he spots it from a mile off. Amazing what food can do. We then continued our ride. Rufus was waiting for me at the stables to find out how I'd got on. When I told him, he said he didn't blame me as it's happened to him too. He said that at this time of year, young cows are let out of their shed for the first time after the winter, and they go all funny. Probably like I did when I ate all that lovely fresh grass.

This is Smartie. I think she's the most beautiful pony I've ever seen. I don't know what to say to her when she's in my field. She's so beautiful that I find it difficult to talk to her. All I can blurt out when I'm in her presence is that we are the same colour, but I don't have a stripe down my back or tiger marks on my legs like her. She acknowledges me, but that's it. Normally she has Benny, Timothy and Teddy all around her. They are really experienced with children and I've only had Carolyn on my back. Smartie must think me so young and inexperienced. I haven't said anything to Rufus, but he must have noticed that whenever Smartie is about, I go all fuzzy. When Rufus and I are chatting, he will just drop into the conversation that one day I'll be so experienced that many girls will want to graze by me. But I don't want anyone else, only Smartie.

This is Major with his favourite food, cow parsley. And a picture of his beautiful moustache. Major is the only one in the stables to have a moustache (except for Beauty, but we'll skip over that).

Carolyn bought him from Llanybedder horse sales when he was three years old. He's now 13 years old. His name was Rocky when he came, but Major seemed to suit him better. He was telling Rufus and me in the field last night (Major always likes to take centre stage) that morale in the horse field hasn't been great recently. He said it was great at first, lots of sun on our backs, eating lovely grass, and lazing around, but you can have too much of a good thing. Major said that when anything is there constantly, it stops being a treat. He told us he took charge of the situation.

'As you all know, that's the position I hold,'
Major told us. 'Every morning, Carolyn comes
to chat with us, and as she was leaving today,
I followed her to the gate and started
pushing it. Carolyn understood. So as a result
of my actions, two of us now come to the
stables for a few days to feel we're still
needed and are useful. We did have a breakout
one day. I bet you can guess who it was — yes
Teddy (he's from the valleys and can break
out of anywhere) and his sidekick Bluebell.
They walked back to the stables, stopping on
the way to eat cow parsley.'

After Major had finished holding
court, Rufus and I looked at each
other and thought how lucky we are
to have lessons each day. I'll try to
remember what Major told us if I ever
get fed up with lessons. Rufus says just
eating and sleeping is not good for the soul.

This week I'm practising with my driving harness. It's to get me used to my second bridle with blinkers on. It's taking me a while to adjust to it. I can't see behind me because the blinkers restrict my vision. I'm getting better each day, as I trust Carolyn and listen to her voice. Goodness knows what she's talking about sometimes, but I guess she thinks it helps me. To be honest, it probably does.

Today, Carolyn has been making all sorts of weird noises behind me (I don't think it has anything to do with the curry she ate last night!). It does scare me but I'm getting braver each day. Rufus told me that Carolyn won't push my lessons onto harder ones until I'm really happy with what I am doing. Rufus said that unless you can work out a situation, it will worry you, and that's no way to learn. I asked Rufus why I need blinkers. He said he would explain later. Does that mean he doesn't know?

We did it, we did it!
I'm on such a high.
Rufus and I went out
for a ride together.
Can you believe that?
My bestest friend
and me. Going for
a ride up the hill.
We met a car on the
way, but Rufus went
by without a care,
so I did the same.
When you have a
great friend, who
is so experienced

and wise, you follow in their hoof steps.
Thank goodness Tiggy was not my mentor. I will get
around to telling you about her one day... She can be a
little naughty, to say the least. She 'doesn't suffer fools
gladly' – whatever that means.

Meditation morning. I refuse to join in all these classes.
They're for the more 'mature ' ones. Guess who's in charge
of them all? Yes, Major. I bet he hopes his name is going
to be changed to Sergeant Major. In today's class there
was Harry Potter (he goes to all the classes), Buster and
Rufus. A small class today. They met in the top field
because it's got lovely views and Rufus said you can
feel the 'yang and yin'(?). Don't ask! Rufus said these
classes are good for your body and soul in these times.
Rufus doesn't push me to go to the classes as he knows
they don't interest me one jot. What's the point of just
lying down in the field, focusing on a piece of grass?
Joe isn't allowed to go to this class as he would just eat.
He should go to the exercise classes, though. They're all
saying, 'Joe looks well'. We all know what that means!

I asked Rufus if he thought Carolyn would find a child for me to have fun with. He said they're a bit thin on the ground at the moment (I just nod when he says odd things like that, not a clue what he means!). Carolyn and I went for a lovely long walk today. I had my driving harness on, so I could get used to my blinkers, which I'm not over the moon about.

The hedgerows were beautiful. We called at Carolyn's friend Cathy's house. They talked and talked and talked. You'd think they never saw anyone. Oh, maybe in these times that's probably true.

A dog lives there called Monty. He's a very clever dog, because when he feels hungry, he follows the chickens round and when they lay an egg, he eats it. The egg not the chicken! That would be a very naughty dog if he ate the chicken.

I went to my first show yesterday. I know you'll all say there are no shows due to lockdown. But this was virtual! How crazy is that? I didn't get nervous or need to be groomed (shame) as the picture that was sent clearly indicates. It

was run by the Glamorgan WPCS (work that one out for yourselves Rufus told me). Needless to say, I came nowhere. But as Rufus says, it's the taking part that counts. Rufus said that if anyone asks me if I have competed at a show, I can honestly say yes. So when prima donna Cocoa asks if I have been to a show, I will say yes, I have.

Rufus said that when he went to his first show, he won a second place rosette. 'That was amazing,' I said. Then I asked a question I shouldn't have asked. 'How many were in the class?' I don't think he heard me as he carried on eating.

I wish you all a good morning. I (Rufus) have been requested by the young Horace to tell you of his ordeal yesterday. He still feels a little shaken up. I will start at the beginning. (I can hear Horace saying, 'where else would you start?'.) Yesterday, Carolyn put his driving harness on. He's had his driving harness on all week and was getting more used to the blinkers. But unfortunately, a small string of events happened and he got scared. If it had just been one thing, he would have coped. I know Horace, and he would have been brave and stepped up to the mark. I will tell you what he said to me when he returned to the field after that fateful day. Then I will need to translate, as it will soon become clear to you how quickly he was talking when you read on.

'Oh no it was just so awful the wall jumped out and hit me on my shoulder I was just getting over that then a gate hit me on my bum and I tried to run away from it all and turned and looked at everything attacking me from behind but couldn't see because of the horrible blinkers I was scared a lion would jump on my back...'

At this point I stopped him, as his imagination was really running away with him. As I said, I will translate.

We'll take it a step at a time. His lesson was going very well, when apparently he decided to take a shorter route than Carolyn had asked him to. In doing so, he brushed his shoulder against the wall and as he had his blinkers on, he didn't see it, so it gave him a big fright. If he'd done what Carolyn had asked, all would have been well. He's getting to the point where he knows what to do. Nothing wrong with that, it shows he's gaining more confidence.

Horace recovered from that little incident, but unfortunately Carolyn then opened a gate and led him through. She stopped to look at a flower, and the gate slammed shut, hitting his backside in the process. That was the straw that broke the camel's back. Panic set in. Carolyn led him back to the stables, took off his blinkers and put his ordinary bridle back on. She continued with his lesson and all was well.

But he was still shaken up. Carolyn will now take things very slowly regarding the blinkers, but will continue full swing with his riding and general education.

I don't know where the lion jumping on his back came from. Maybe it was Benny telling his stories and jokes to everyone in the field? Young ones can be so impressionable, I may have a quiet word with Benny. Well, that's my job done. I have no doubt at all that Horace will be back to his happy-go-lucky self tomorrow.

Regards,

Rufus

I would like to start by thanking Rufus for standing in and writing my diary. I was a bit out of sorts yesterday. After reading through Rufus's account, I realised that I had over reacted. But at the time everything was very frightening. It's amazing how wise we are after the event. But as Rufus has told me, you have to face many frightening things in your life which you have to deal with. It makes you stronger and teaches you how to get through difficulties.

I've just come back from a lovely ride up the hill with Carolyn and Birtie. We saw the mountains that Rufus has told me about. Maybe next week I'll ride up there. I'm back!

Hello, anyone about? Hello. Where are Carolyn and Birtie? Everything is even more quiet than it normally is. Oh, here comes Miss Know–it–all, Carys. She so loves a bit of gossip. Rufus always tells me to take everything that she says with a pinch of salt. (I don't think I'd like salt, never had it. Rufus always talks in riddles.)

Anyway, Carys couldn't help herself, out it gushed. 'You'll never guess what Carolyn did last night! She ate a raw egg, followed by a spoon of sugar and then neat gin! I bet she's not well today and that's why she's not here.'

Rufus turned to me and said, 'See, I told you not to listen to a word Carys says, Carolyn would never do something so stupid.' We heard later that it was true! Carolyn did it for an NHS challenge to raise money.

She's so beautiful. I can't keep my eyes off her. Tiggy (what a glorious name) arrived in the field next door to mine four days ago. I have stood looking over this fence since then. I find doing my lessons is a real inconvenience. Can't Carolyn see I'm doing something? What's the point of doing lessons when my mind is not on the job?

My senses are a lot sharper. I'm finding my lessons feel a little longer, and sometimes I puff a little. I must say it then makes me concentrate a little more on my lesson. But as soon as I'm finished, I'm back looking at this beautiful goddess. Rufus has told me to get a grip. I'm sure whatever that means is not what I want to hear. I told Rufus that Tiggy is the one for me. He muttered, 'You said that about Smartie, Cocoa and Carys, to mention but a few.' But this is the one.

Stretch. And one, two, three, hold it. And relax. Let's do that again. You at the back there. Yes you, Joe. You should be really putting your back into this. Just look at yourself, you have really let yourself go. Take this seriously. Now take up your position again. Stretch. This is 'Major's morning workout', or more like, 'Do as you're told or I will bellow at you'!

Rufus joins in religiously. I've only tried it once. I have a great excuse not to do it, because I have to do my lessons with Carolyn. Even if I don't have a lesson that day, I make myself scarce. How boring exercises are. Especially with old Sergeant Major shouting at you. Don't get me wrong, it's very good for the oldies and the ones that have over indulged in lockdown, but I'm too young for any of that stuff. Like meditation mornings. Rufus said it's good for the mind. Well, my mind is fine, thank you very much. Can't we have race round the field games or who can jump the highest tree? That's would be my sort of workout.

Last night Rufus and I were chewing the cud discussing lockdown. (Odd term isn't it? We're not cows, although we do have one at the stables, because every spring she turns into one.) We decided to list our positives and negatives. Rufus said his life hasn't drastically changed. He's become my mentor (not sure if that is a positive or a negative for him!). The stables are so much quieter. It's sad not having the hustle and bustle about the place, although to start with it was pleasant. But now, no more carrots that people used to bring.

Rufus said that we've had it a lot better than the other ponies, because they only have the company of whoever is in the field with them. They said it was good to start with, but now they're very bored and getting fed up with everyone in their field. The only light relief is Major's morning classes. Now that must be desperation! Rufus asked me what my positives and negatives were. I said I needed to think about it. I would write a list tonight. We can then keep it and compare it to how our lives are in two month's time.

Just a little higher, oh that's the spot. I'm in heaven. Just what friends are for. You scratch me, I'll scratch you. Rufus asked how I was getting on with my negatives and positives list for lockdown. I stayed up late last night writing it. Here we go.

Negatives
1. None.

Positives
1. Learning how to be ridden
2. Being groomed every day
3. Being part of the stables
4. Feeling fit and in good shape
5. Having Rufus as my bestest friend.

I'm learning to open and shut gates. Not literally me, but Carolyn while she's riding me. And I'm getting used to lots of bikes going past me. Most of the bike riders are great. They shout or ring their bell to say they're behind so I can prepare myself. But some are like ghosts, they silently creep up on you, then zoom by. It scares me a little. But I'm getting braver.

Because I'm going on longer rides now, Birtie the dog doesn't come. He gets put away in the house, which he hates. Rufus said he nearly died two years ago! 'What happened?' I asked Rufus. He said he would tell me tonight before I go to bed. I'm going on a night ride through the woods tonight. It's going to be scary but exciting all at once. Will tell you all about it tomorrow.

Last night's ride in the woods was amazing. I can't believe I was allowed to go because it really was my bedtime. It was nearly dark when we got back. I got scared a few times because the shadows moved on the ground and I thought they would jump up at me. But Buster led the way to give me confidence. I was on such a high when I got back. I was so hungry. I was too excited to go to sleep, so Rufus told me the story of Birtie.

Rufus said that two years ago, Birtie caught a rat and it had been poisoned. Birtie got very ill. Carolyn carried him to the vet. The vet said the only way he would live would be a blood transfusion. Carolyn asked her friend Lynda, who breeds some very swanky Labradors, if she could borrow one. Llanstinan Rosie bravely gave her blood. Birtie came home three days later, but couldn't use his back legs. Everyone was so happy he was home. But it was still touch and go if he pulled through. He was still very weak, but insisted he go out to the stables with Carolyn every day. He was carried out and wrapped up while he watched the lessons going on. He even had a man called Andrew massage his legs to make them better. After a few weeks, Birtie started improving, and now you wouldn't be able to tell how ill he was.

Wow, what a story! So Birtie is half girl Labrador? Yes, Rufus said. Birtie is very proud that he has top show blood in him, and he loves telling his girlfriend's that he's in touch with his feminine side!

Rufus and I have been standing tucked up by the hedge today. It's rather cold and wet. No lessons today! It gives one time to reflect on the week that has just gone by. Some good things and one little bad thing. Well, at the time I thought it would be a bit of fun. You know the saying 'in hindsight'? It happened two days ago.

Carolyn was bringing four of us in from the field. She was leading Nina and Harry Potter, but left me and Rufus to follow. Which we always do. Normally. But I don't know what took possession of me: the sun on my back, the wind in my mane, or showing off to the girls, I'm not sure. I decided to trot off by myself up the road. It was great fun. Amazingly, Rufus followed. At the time, I was sure Rufus was saying 'Go, go'. So I went faster. But he was actually shouting 'No, no'. Oh dear. I just thought this was fun. I got carried away and turned the corner and went for it. I then spotted some cow parsley growing in the hedge and stopped to eat. Carolyn eventually caught me up, puffing a lot.

I do think it's time she joined in Major's exercise classes. I'm sure it would benefit her. But I think that would have been a bad moment to mention it. Carolyn was a tiny weeny bit annoyed with me. And of course, poor Rufus also got the blame for my high jinks. Rufus said, 'Worse things happen at sea.' There he goes again with these strange sayings. Totally unrelated.

Apart from that, my lessons have been going well. We did a long ride one day through Tycanol woods, so the following day we did ride and lead. Me being led with no one on my back.

And a bit of news, Major has added some new exercise classes to jazz things up a bit, as his class numbers were falling. Tennis has been included.

I've got to go now as it's stopped raining so I can get some good eating time in. Until tomorrow.

Last night Carolyn put us in a field full of wonderful rich grass. So that's what I'm blaming it on. It wasn't my fault that I didn't want to do my exercise today, although Rufus begs to differ. Today I treated Carolyn as if I was the leader of the herd. I tried to take control. Wrong move. When she was putting my saddle on, I put my ears back, only just a little bit, and tried to nip her very gently. Oh dear, I got a little smack on my nose. That put me in my place straight away. I've never ever thought of doing that before, and now I'll never ever think of doing it again.

Rufus told me that we are a pack animals, and we have to have a leader. Carolyn is our leader. She will never put you in a position that you won't be able to understand or be ready to cope with. But she will assert her authority if you overstep the mark (which I learnt today!). Rufus said that I'm learning boundaries. The same happens when you're in the field herd. A horse will be the leader. Like Buster or Bluebell for instance. You don't argue with them, you follow them. When you understand this, it makes you become a nicer pony. Well mannered and kind. Then all the children will want to ride you.

After that lesson, I could do no wrong! We did lots of trotting. Discovering a new track. I really enjoyed my ride out. And to finish off, Carolyn rode me round the sand school for the first time. It's amazing how my attitude changed after that little disagreement!

Not naming names, but those two must stop eating and join Major's exercise class. They've really let themselves go in lockdown.

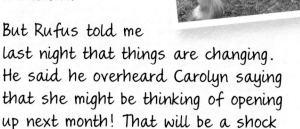

But Rufus told me last night that things are changing. He said he overheard Carolyn saying that she might be thinking of opening up next month! That will be a shock to those fatties and Carolyn. Rufus said it will be very good for me, because a lot more will be going on around the stables. I do have a problem with different noises, and that worries me. Rufus said if I had lots of hustle and bustle going on around me all the time, I would become desensitised to it. If Rufus says so, then it must right.

There is talk that Carolyn will be doing her annual night ride over the mountains this week. I wonder who she will ride? I could try, although I would be tired after. Nothing that a day off wouldn't solve. I've got young legs and have shown that I can carry a huge weight. When I'm being ridden I don't tire, it's only when I go back to the field that I have to have a sleep.

'Is it true, what Carys told me?' I asked Rufus.

'Oh no, what has she been saying now?'

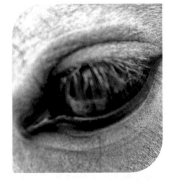

'She said that because I have one blue eye, I will get laughed at when I go to a show.'

Rufus sighed and said, 'You know you mustn't pay attention to Carys at certain times of the month. She can't help it. I've told you before that it doesn't matter what colour you are, how you walk or stand, how big or small you are. What matters is your attitude to others. You are a kind, considerate, happy, pony. If you show that to others, you will receive it back. When you go to a show, you do your best with what you've been born with. That will shine through and ponies will respect you for that and treat you equally.'

I thanked Rufus. Carys can be really great sometimes but awful at other times. I'll have to learn to graze away from her when there's a full moon.

I have actually done it! It's wonderful when you have dreamed of something and it comes true. I've been to the mountain! When I started my training, going to the mountain seemed so unattainable. But as Rufus says, 'Dream, work hard and be happy, and you will get there. It may take time but don't give up.'

I must say that at times the mountain looked so very far away, but with my bestest friend Rufus encouraging me, I've managed it. It was lovely on the mountain. I can't wait to go on a picnic ride there and eat all the grass. I bet it has a different flavour to the grass in my field.

On a different note, excessive eating. Major is trying his best with Joe to get him to exercise. But I feel it's a losing battle. Major has been trying to do a one-to-one keep fit lesson with Joe, in the hope that Joe would make an effort. Major has developed this new exercise program where you lie on your back and stretch your legs in the air (at the moment, Carys would be good at that). But Joe just looks down at him lying on the ground. We all know that if you have no interest in something, being ordered to do it won't help matters. I'm sure when lessons and ride outs restart, Joe will shed pounds (or it might have to be stones in his case). I'm sure all will work out in the end.

Things are starting to change at the stables. Rufus said it's like the gathering of the clan. Rufus said it happens every year, but usually at Easter time. Because of lockdown, everything is very different this year. All the horses and ponies are arriving at the stables. There's an excited feel about the place. Old friends, who have been apart since the start of winter, are meeting up.

I'm excited, as Rufus said he had overheard Carolyn saying that children were booking for lessons already. I don't think children will ride me this year as I'm not experienced enough, but I'm sure I will be groomed a lot. A vet is coming to check everyone's health (not Birtie or Carolyn) to make sure they can be ridden. Apparently, Beauty stands by the vet to assist him. It will be my first time checked by a vet. I've only seen one once before, when I was a foal, to have a microchip put in my neck. (It stung a bit, but my mum was by my side.)

I hope I have kept you entertained over lockdown and kept you in contact with the stables. Goodbye for now.

Horace.

THE END

– or is it just the beginning!